9 Things a Leader MUST DO

DR. HENRY CLOUD

Published by
THOMAS NELSON™
Since 1798

www.thomasnelson.com

9 Things a Leader Must Do

Copyright © 2006 by Henry Cloud

Published in Nashville, Tennessee, by Thomas Nelson, Inc.

Published in association with Yates & Yates, LLP Attorneys and Literary Agents, Orange, California.

Cover Design: The DesignWorks Group
Interior Design: VisibilityCreative.com

Library of Congress Cataloging-in-Publication Data

Cloud, Henry.
9 Things a Leader Must Do/Henry Cloud.
p. cm.
Summary: "A simple roadmap to help leaders, and those who want to become
leaders, arrive at greater levels of personal growth and corporate
influence"–Provided by publisher.

ISBN-13: 978-1-59145-484-7 (hardcover)
ISBN-10: 1-59145-484-0 (hardcover)

1. Leadership–Religious aspects–Christianity. 2. Leadership. 3.
Leaders–Religious life. I. Title. II. Title: Nine things a leader must do.

BV4597.53.L43C56 2006
158'.4–dc22
2006021309

Printed in the United States of America
07 08 09 QW 6 5 4

CONTENTS

9 THINGS A LEADER MUST DO

FOREWORD

One of the things I admire about Henry Cloud is his passion for helping others. His books and speaking have improved the lives of so many people. He is successful and he reaches out to others to help them become successful—emotionally, spiritually, and professionally.

I have been studying and teaching leadership my entire adult life. I can see that as one of the foremost experts on relationships, Henry brings a unique and compelling perspective to the topic of leadership. His observations come from the heart and are rooted in his interaction with people—many of whose stories he shares in this book.

I especially appreciate that Henry looks at leadership from the inside out and includes his signature message of taking ownership for who we are and how we interact with others. And he provides specific actions we can take to grow and improve in each of the nine areas he presents.

As you read with an open heart and mind, I pray that with God's help you will go to the next level—and take others with you. That, after all, is what leadership is all about.

John C. Maxwell

INTRODUCTION

DÉJÀ VU LEADERS

It seemed like I was stuck in a rerun of *The X-Files* or *The Twilight Zone.* I would be in a business meeting or a consulting situation or the company of other individuals who had in some way distanced themselves from the pack when it came to success in business. I would think, *Wait a minute…I've met this person before.* But I knew I was meeting the individual for the first time.

But the experience kept repeating itself. Each time it had that familiar ring of *I know you from somewhere* in the presence of a new acquaintance. At least they reminded me of someone I had known before. But who could it be?

Then one day I noticed something. I was working on a business deal, and a particular situation came up. One of my friends in the deal said he would take care of the thing we were discussing. He offered a way of handling it, and we moved on to the next issue. But I had that same feeling of déjà vu about what was going on. *Why does this seem so familiar?* I asked myself.

Then it hit me. What I felt had nothing to do with my friend or with anyone else in the room. *It had to do with what my friend did.* It was the way he handled the situation. That's what I had seen before. I had seen someone else do that same thing only a week earlier. The man I was with at the moment and the person I had been with the week before, in similar circumstances and facing a similar dilemma, had responded in exactly the same way. *It was as if all these people were the same person, in a way.*

But here is the interesting thing, and the thing that added to the confusion: All these people were very different from one another. A good number of them were in business or other arenas of leadership, but they had different backgrounds, different personalities, different economic circumstances, and different abilities. However, they were the same in that they shared this particular way of handling life and work. And that commonality, I realized, was the déjà vu I kept experiencing.

THREE REALIZATIONS

As I reflected upon the people who possessed this pattern of behavior in common, something else became evident: *They were all successful in what they did.* They moved forward. They did not stay stuck in the same mistakes over and over again. They reached their goals and found what they were looking for in their work and lives. There must be a connection, I thought, with their success and this pattern that I kept observing. Pondering this phenomenon, three realizations came into focus for me.

Realization number one: The answer to "Who is this person?" was not a person at all. It was a way of behaving. I realized that I was not looking at a person; I was looking at a pattern. A way of behaving. Now that I recognized the pattern, I decided to look for it even more. A path that successful leaders took, given a certain set of choices.

Realization number two: People who found what they were looking for in life seemed to do a certain set of things in common. I began to identify several ways of behaving and responding that successful leaders had in common—ways they handled themselves, their relationships, their work, and their lives. There was no identifiable personality type common to these people. Rather, there were *several* identifiable ways that these people did business and lived life, and for the most part they all practiced them.

Realization number three: If you were not born with these patterns for leadership in place, you can learn them. After looking at these people over and over again, it was clear to me that they got these principles from different places—family, mentors, therapy, seeking, spiritual awakening, disaster, and so on. There was no consistent pattern for acquiring them that I could put my finger on. But that said something greater than if I had found a special history they all shared. Since there was nothing in common about these people's background or IQ, these patterns did not reside in any one type of person. These patterns transcend all backgrounds, talents, and limitations.

Thus, *they exist on their own and are available to all of us.* They are not things that one person "possesses" and another does not, like a talent. Instead, we can all learn these patterns that work every time and lead to better lives. My firm belief is that once you do learn this pattern, your life and the lives of those you lead will never be the same.

NINE THINGS DÉJÀ VU LEADERS DO

This pattern of behavior that I discovered in déjà vu leaders, these Nine Things every leader must do, are kind of like gravity. Even though you can't see it, gravity exists. Cooperate with it and it will help you do great things. Even fly. Ignore gravity and you will fall and hurt yourself. In the same way, these Nine Things are there, and we can work with them to achieve great results in business, relationships, and other areas of life. Or we can ignore them and suffer the consequences.

Now, I would not say that my particular way of communicating these Nine Things is as certain as the proven laws of physics. But what I would say with confidence is this: Working with a lot of people and practicing these Nine Things myself has shown them to be utterly dependable. I am convinced that you can count on them to help you avoid hitting the pavement. In the upcoming chapters, we will see where they come from, how they work, how to put them into practice, and the pitfalls of not following them.

I chose these Nine Things for three specific reasons.

First, they are paths or patterns of behavior that really do make a huge difference in the lives and leadership of those who practice them. I consider them uncontainable in their fruitfulness.

Second, avoiding these principles can lead to disastrous consequences, such as a loss of dreams, goals, potential, relationships, profits, market share, trust—even faith itself.

Third, these principles are often ignored. I seldom hear them talked about as specific patterns to be observed and diligently applied.

Wise King Solomon admonishes, "Hold onto instruction, do not let it go; guard it well, for it is your life" (Proverbs 4:13). These Nine Things are wisdom, principles God himself has set in place for us to learn. In this book we will look at this wisdom in the lives and experiences of what I call "déjà vu leaders" to see how it can instruct us. What we gain will help us to find more and more of the success we were created to enjoy.

Let's jump in now and look at the nine principles to learn how they can help you lead with ever increasing success.

1

EXCAVATE YOUR SOUL

THING ONE

Déjà vu leaders explore their deep hearts
and invest in their inner desires and drives

Many years ago, a little girl just under the age of two was playing in the den before bedtime. She picked up a couple of blocks and stacked one on top of another. Then she added another block, and then another. Something sparked inside her. She was so excited to see the tower of blocks she had built.

Mommy and Daddy noticed too, and their excitement matched hers. "That's so good, Susie!" they exclaimed. Everyone was enjoying the moment, but what was really happening was much more than a moment's joy. It was a miracle. For Susie was discovering two of the most powerful forces in the universe: the talent and desire God had planted deep within her.

In preschool and kindergarten, Susie spent hours drawing and painting in art class. When she took the pencil or brush in her hand, something special happened. Not only did it provide a different level of enjoyment than soccer, but her teachers noticed it and encouraged her with every drawing.

As her schooling continued, Susie found the same kind of attraction to her math classes—an attraction she lacked in literature and English. Her parents not only encouraged her interests but helped her when she struggled and taught her the value of hard work and study. As a result, Susie graduated from college with honors, went on to graduate school, and became what she had dreamed of becoming since high school: a highly successful architect. I've conducted seminars in the arena Susie designed, and it is magnificent. And it all began in the tiny heart of a toddler.

Dig up Your Heart's Desire

Everything we see around us in the visible world, including Susie's arena, began in the invisible world of someone's soul. It was first a talent, then a dream. It came into being because of discipline and desire, all invisible ingredients which live in the souls of men and women. For successful leaders, the invisible world is where the visible world originates. What lies deep inside is where the real life is.

The same is true at all levels of leadership in the business world. Every blockbuster deal, every new rung on the corporate ladder, every project design, every company merger, and every successful sales campaign begins in the invisible soul of human beings. Leadership success is the process of digging up the treasures of the invisible soul in order to bring dreams, desires, and talents into the visible world. So the first thing déjà vu leaders do to succeed is

*to listen to their hearts and invest
in their inner desires and drives.*

In order to optimize his opportunities in business and life, the déjà vu leader:

- Becomes aware of his dreams, desires, talents, and other treasures of the soul.

- Listens to them and values them as life itself.

- Takes steps to develop them, beginning in very small ways.

- Seeks coaching and help to make them grow.

- Does not care as much about his results as his essence, but just continues to express his soul-treasures wherever he can.

FIND THE BURIED TREASURE

So why don't we seek this internal life? Because we all have experiences that make our internal life unavailable to us. For example, some people didn't have observant and encouraging parents like Susie did. Their family may have severely dampened any sense of inner drive and inspiration. As a result, they find themselves living lives that are out of touch with the very center of life itself: with their hearts, minds, and souls.

Deeply exploring your soul means that you must face some fears and obstacles. What caused you to bury your treasure? Was it a harsh parent? A tough relationship? A lack of opportunity or resources that caused you to give up? A subculture that put you down? Other people who did not like what you brought forth from inside your heart and soul? The times you tried and failed?

One thing is sure:

*there is no shortage of things in this life
that can cause you to bury your heart and soul.*

The truth is, however, that those who succeed in business or any aspect of leadership and life have not allowed those influences to keep their dreams and desires hidden. They have dug them out, faced their fears, taken risks, failed, gotten up again, and found that they could indeed build something magnificent.

Julia was such a person. When she was in her early twenties, she fell in love and married Devin, a "winner"—the type of person who knew who he was and where he was going. Devin pursued his career, built a big electronics business, and achieved considerable success. Although Julia had always enjoyed school and directing various service projects, after marriage she quit doing much with her organizational talents. Overshadowed by Devin's drive and aggressiveness, she became more a follower of his career and life.

At first the cause of her withdrawal from the things she enjoyed seemed to be the demands of her role as mother of young children. But there were other causes more subtle. Devin put her down. He had many ways of dominating, but the most harmful were those in which he discounted her abilities. Slowly she retreated into the area where she did not have to compete with him: that of being a mother. She performed very well in that role and just put her other talents aside.

As many such stories go, years later Devin became

bored with the woman he had subdued and fell in love with someone from work. He left Julia behind. After the divorce, she did not know what she was going to do. She felt lost.

Her friends would have none of that, however. Some of them knew her before she married Devin and they knew of her outstanding talents and abilities. They pushed her to step out. She resisted, feeling that she was "stupid" and could not really make the kinds of decisions required to do the kinds of work they were telling her to go for. But her friends would not hear of it, so Julia relented, and her friend Molly hired her to work in her company.

Julia was not long in her new job before she began to put her hand to organizing things around there, even beyond her assigned duties. Then she discovered that to help the company as much as she wanted, she needed to acquire some computer skills that she did not possess. The thought both frightened and excited her. So without others knowing it, she took a class at the community college. Gradually, she offered to help on some of the bigger projects at work. Soon employees from other departments turned to her for help. She was gaining a reputation. Not long after, she was moved to a new position in more complicated operations, and within a year she was running a division with big budgets.

As she related her story, Julia said one thing that was quite telling: "I had somehow lost touch with what I liked to do, and slowly I had come to believe that I couldn't do it. It was like a part of me had died. Then, when I thought about doing it again, I was too afraid to try. If it weren't for Molly making me step out and try that little job, I don't know where I would be today."

This choice, I believe, is always put before us, every day. We are given a heart full of treasure and talent, feelings and desires. In short, God has granted to us *potential realities for leadership and success at many levels.* It is our job to dig up whatever potential we have. The choice is whether we are going to allow fear and experiences to keep our potential buried, or choose to step out in faith and see that potential turn into reality.

One of the best examples of this is found in the parable of the talents. In this parable in Matthew 25:14-30, the master entrusts three servants with various amounts of money to be invested while he is away. He returns at a later date and checks out what they have done. Two of the servants stepped out, took risks, were diligent, and earned a handsome profit for the master. The third was afraid and buried his treasure in the ground. He returned only what he was originally given.

The first two were rewarded, and the last one was scolded and lost the little that he had. Is that picture of reality or what? Those who take what they possess, invest it in life, and are diligent and faithful with it over time, grow and build something good. But those who allow fear to keep them from stepping out, *not only fail to increase what they have, they actually lose it.*

As Solomon said about minding what is inside the heart: "Above all else, guard your heart, for it is the wellspring of life" (Proverbs 4:23). *Above all else* is pretty strong language, don't you think? We can see why Solomon uses those words when we realize that without guarding what is inside the heart, no building is ever built, no career is ever born or reborn, no leader ever achieves his or her potential.

His phrase, *wellspring of life,* says it all. It means that place from which it all comes. Success and failure alike arise from what is going on inside, and the wise person is the one who pays attention.

Put on Your Hard Hat— and Take the Appropriate Risks

Julia did not just dig things out of her soul and let them lie there. She took risks to invest her invisible treasures in the visible world. Julia stepped out and tried her skills. With each new victory, she gained more ground in the external world as the interior world of her heart and soul was expanding.

There is very little growth and reward in life without taking risks. As the parable says, the one who buried his treasure in the ground did so to avoid risk of loss, failure, and disapproval. In the end, though, he reaped all three of these disasters. Clearly,

avoidance of risk is the greatest risk of all.

Taking risks, however, does not mean that when you discover a treasure in your heart you should just roll the dice. Julia was diligent and followed her path with wisdom and calculation. She took it one step at a time. As Solomon tells us, "The wisdom of the prudent is to give thought to their ways, but the folly of fools is deception" (Proverbs 14:8).

The déjà vu leader is not afraid of the downside of taking risks. But he does not jump off cliffs and then expect good things to happen. To the contrary, healthy risk is calculated, integrated, and then executed with diligence and thoughtfulness. Most leaders who "left it all," took a risk, and succeeded will tell you that their decision was not flighty or impulsive at all. They made their move only after much preparation and thoughtfulness.

MAKE YOUR INVISIBLE WORLD VISIBLE

In order to get to the outside visible world, your desires and talents have to be mined, refined, and sculpted. You have to own them, work them, and use them. Here are some tips on how to do that:

- Listen to what bugs you. It might be a message.

- Don't let negative feelings just sit there. Do something about them.

- Don't let long-term wishes and dreams go ignored. Find out what they mean.

- Listen to your symptoms. They might be telling you that you have something to dig up.

- Pay attention to your fantasies. They may be telling you that something is missing that you need to resolve in appropriate ways.

- Face the fears and obstacles that have caused you to bury your inner treasures.

- Don't confuse envy with desire. You may be envious of someone else's position or success because you have lost touch with your own dreams.

- Do everything above in the context of your values and the community of people who are committed to guarding your heart. If you do not have such a community, find one and join it.

- Ask God to help you find your heart, mind, soul, and the treasures He has placed there for you.

Often, the biggest sign that tells us of things buried in the heart is numbness and a life that is not alive. Déjà vu leaders will always choose life, and that means their heart, mind, and soul are always getting attention. And when they see those telltale signs, they take action.

Grasp your dreams. Reach for them. Take appropriate risks. One of the worst things you can die with is potential. Potential is something to be realized, not guarded or protected. So, dig it up! Invest it! And you will find that it is true—life comes from the inside out.

2

YANK THE DISEASED TOOTH

THING TWO
*Déjà vu leaders do not allow negative things
to take up space in their lives.*

friend of mine is president of a manufacturing
business with annual sales in the hundreds of
millions of dollars. But the company wasn't
always that size. When he took it over several years ago, it
was about one-sixteenth the size it is now. Even so, it was
still a substantial business with profits into the millions.
All he really had to do in order to be a success was to
keep from screwing things up.

Not only did he not screw things up, my friend put
the company's earnings on steroids. Growth and profits
exploded. One day I asked him how he did it. He said,

"When I first took over, I sold off 80 percent of the company at big losses."

I was shocked. How can a guy gut a profitable company by giving most of it away at a big loss, and then expect it to explode with growth?

My friend went on. "I saw that the *life of the company* was really in about 20 percent of the overall activity. So I kept that 20 percent and sold off the rest of the operations and assets, sometimes at pennies on the dollar—and I did it quickly. I wanted to keep the superfluous stuff from draining focus, energy, resources, and attention away from the good things we had going. And that's what led to our eventual success."

My friend is a shining example of the second principle for successful leadership:

Déjà vu leaders do not allow negative things to take up space in their lives.

If they can't fix the bad stuff, they get rid of it. Sometimes quickly and sometimes through a process, but if a tooth is infected, they yank it out. *They get rid of negative energy.*

CAVITIES TO FILL, TEETH TO PULL

Sometimes this negative energy is generated by the presence of things that are truly negative, such as a significant unresolved problem with a project or a coworker. These are major negatives, bad stuff. At other times the negative energy comes from things that are not innately bad, but simply are not best for the person involved. These are minor negatives that distract you from those deepest desires in your heart or the most important things in life. But they can spoil your dreams as readily as the big stuff.

The apostle Paul told the Corinthians, "'Everything is permissible for me'—but I will not be mastered by anything" (1 Corinthians 6:12). He was determined not to let even things that were okay have control over him in any way. Even good things that consume time, resources, energy, and attention and do not get you where you want to go are a negative. Déjà vu leaders fill the cavities in the minor bad stuff and yank out the major bad stuff.

Examples of negative energy in a leader's life can be physical (such as the junk that piles up on your desk or in your computer files), relational (such as people who are a bad influence on you), and emotional (such as unnecessary anxiety or worry). We need to clear out clutter, dead weight, things we keep around that don't help us but take up space or drain resources. Get rid of the things you are not using.

Maybe you can relate to a few other examples.

- Relationships that are not going anywhere, or are even taking you places opposite of where you want to go.

- Activities at work or home that are not getting you where you want to go.

- Things you own or are paying for that you are not using, or that are not bringing you true and lasting benefit.

- Time you are spending that is not contributing to your well-being or mission as a leader.

Either fill the cavity or pull the tooth. And the sooner the better. Then new energy, resources, time, and space become available to you to focus on the things that, as my friend said, have *life* in them. The negative energy drain is stopped, making room for the good stuff.

Sometimes the negative is not fixable, and you have to give up on repairing it and toss it out. That may mean letting go of the expectation that something particular can be improved, such as a product line, a department in the company, an employee on probation, or even a pretty good idea. If you know that investing more time toward reaching a solution is never going to help, then it's time to pull the plug and move on. Forget repairing it or changing it. Let it go.

THE PAIN OF BRAIN DRAIN

Another troublesome aspect of allowing negative things to continue past their time is the way the mind deals with them. Think about it. When do you worry about plaguing, avoided, unresolved negative issues? The answer for most of us: when you can do the least about them. When we avoid facing things directly, they tend to grab us at the times when we cannot address them effectively. For example:

- The financial issue you have avoided at the office pops into your mind the moment you lay your head on the pillow or when you wake up in the middle of the night.

- The character issues of your nineteen-year-old son that have bugged you for years are not faced until he flunks out of college or gets sent home for drug abuse.

- Your tendency to commit to activities you don't like brings up resentment when it's time to attend them, but you don't do anything to get out of them.

- The job you hate but are holding on to for no good reason causes frustration as you drive to work every day.

- Working on a project with the employee that you know you should have fired last year makes you angry.

So, here is the sad result of not living like a déjà vu leader: You get the negative emotion of all your problems without the benefits of solving them. Avoidance is really not helping anything, because you still expend the energy and feel the hurt. If you had simply yanked the bad tooth when it started bothering you, you would be over the pain by now. Avoidance always prolongs pain.

WHEN TO CALL THE DENTIST

One of the toughest things to figure out is when to let go of something that is important to you. When do you finally give up on a project, an employee, a goal, or an action plan that just isn't working? Short answer: when all hope for the desired outcome has been exhausted.

Hope is one of the great virtues in life, right up there with faith and love (1 Corinthians 13:13). But hope is not a fairy tale wish; it is bedrock, and you should be able to order your life with it at your side. Hope means investing time and energy toward results that you have solid reason to believe can be achieved. It is not hope to invest time and energy in a goal that has no forces acting upon it to bring it about. That is stagnation. It is a waste of time, and time is ultimately what your life and work are about.

Pulling the tooth—getting rid of the painful problem—has the added benefit of making room for a positive alternative. In fact,

new things that actually have hope for the future cannot appear until you get rid of what was taking up the space that the new thing needs.

If there is no hope for whatever it is you are clinging to, let go of it so you can be open to something new and life-giving.

THE CRINGE FACTOR

There is another way that the déjà vu leader deals with negative problems and energy drains that is even more effective than fixing them or pulling the tooth: *not getting into them to begin with.*

I went to visit a wise friend and advisor several years ago when I was trying to decide from among several options of what to do next in my life. One option looked very good and had tremendous potential for good things. The only problem, as I explained to my friend, was that the person I would be working with had "issues." He had a reputation among people he has worked with of making them feel used.

My advisor looked at me and said, "Why would you want to work with *him?*"

"Well," I said, "that's the downside of the deal. He has a lot of good points. I just have to swallow hard about being connected with him."

My friend said, "I am old enough now and have enough experience that I just don't do any deal or work with anyone where the *cringe factor* is involved."

"What's the cringe factor?" I asked.

"It's that big gulp you would have to take to go forward," he explained. "My rule is this: Anytime I have to cringe or take a big gulp to agree to do anything substantial with anyone, whether to hire him, work with him, or anything significant, I don't do it. Period."

The cringe factor has become a guiding factor for me ever since. And because I heeded this advice, I am not tethered to the person we were discussing, and that means it's not a tooth to pull.

So the lesson here is that the best way to fix a problem is not to have it in the first place. Learn and listen to the little voice inside that tells you things like:

- *This doesn't quite feel right.*

- *I don't feel comfortable doing this or agreeing to this.*

- *This is not what I really want.*

- *This violates an important value.*

- *I'm going to resent this for a long time.*

- *I wish this were not happening.*

Solomon gives us a great proverb about the cringe factor: "A prudent man sees danger and takes refuge, but the simple keep going and suffer for it" (Proverbs 22:3).

If you encounter a situation that you would not want to live with, fix it before you go forward, or don't go forward without realizing that you are choosing to live with a bad tooth. An ounce of prevention is worth a million pounds of cure.

Unresolved negative things have no place in a leader's heart. This principle does not negate patience, longsuffering, hope, or working out difficult relationships over time. Do whatever you can to fix what is wrong and make it better. Forgive and reconcile. But don't let bad situations sit, stagnate, get infected, and drain your life away. "A cheerful heart is good medicine, but a crushed spirit dries up the bones" (Proverbs 17:22). Move quickly to deal with whatever is crushing your spirit.

3

PLAY THE WHOLE MOVIE

THING THREE

Déjà vu leaders evaluate their decisions in the present based on how they will affect the future.

An old man sat down on his favorite bench—just as he did each day—for his lunchtime ritual of reading the newspaper. Leafing through the pages, the old man noticed a young man sit down at the other end of his bench with a newspaper of his own and begin reading.

After a few minutes, the young man said, "Excuse me, sir. Would you happen to have the time?"

The old man looked the young man over for a moment. "No," he said, then went back to reading his paper.

Puzzled, the young man said, "Sir, I don't mean to be a pest, but I see that you are wearing a watch. Yet when I asked you for the time, you said no. Have I offended you in some way?"

The old man eyed him up and down. "No, not at all," he said finally. Then he went back to his paper.

"But I don't understand," the young man said. "Why won't you give me the time?"

The old man put his paper down.

"Well, when you first sat down, I noticed you. You seem like a nice enough young man, clean cut and all. You seem interested in the world and its current events, as I noticed by the particular paper you are reading. Then you asked me for the time. And I figured if I gave you it to you, we might strike up a conversation, and you would probably tell me about yourself, and I would probably like you and we would become friends.

"Then, I would probably invite you to my house sometime to meet my family. If that happened, you would meet my wonderful daughter whom I love very much. She would probably like you, and you would probably like her too. So, the two of you would likely become friends, and then go out on a date. And if that happened, chances are you would fall in love and get married. And I'll be hanged if I'm going to let my daughter marry any man who doesn't own a watch!"

Go to the Movies

The principle we're talking about now is this:

> *Déjà vu leaders evaluate their decisions in the present based on how those decisions affect the future.*

They rarely take any action without considering its future implications. Tell a man the time and you might just end up marrying off your daughter to a guy who doesn't own a watch. Life is a slippery slope!

You never know exactly what might happen down the line when you make a given choice, but the wise person at least thinks about it. However, déjà vu leaders don't just think about future implications when making those big, scary decisions. They tend to think that way all the time, in matters large and small. Successful leaders know how each scene contributes to the film's good end. They don't see just one scene; they watch the whole movie to the end.

The simplest way to look at this principle is a matter of cause and effect. "If I do A, then B will happen." But that doesn't illustrate the profound nature of it. Experience takes us much farther than that. It's more like this: *If I do A, not only will B happen, but C will too. And D and E and F and G and on and on.*

This is the difference between cause and effect and the deeper version of true sowing and reaping. Sowing and reaping is much bigger than the connection between what I am doing now and what will occur immediately following. It's about what I will *ultimately* end up with if I sow this particular behavior, choice, attitude, value, or strategy. It is the long-term view. More accurately, it is the end view. *What will happen in the end?* is the question the wise leader seeks to answer.

Déjà vu leaders evaluate almost everything they do in this way. They see every behavior and decision as links in a larger chain, steps in a direction that has a destination. And they see these links in both directions, the good *and* the bad. They think this way to attain the good things they want in life and to avoid the bad things they don't want. In short, they rarely do anything without thinking of the ultimate consequences. They play the whole movie, so to speak.

Any one thing you do is only a scene in a larger movie. To understand a particular action, you have to play it out all the way to the end of the movie. After viewing the entire film, you can decide whether you really want that scene in the movie of your life. If it alters the plot of your story, or takes you to other scenes you don't want to live out, or even causes the movie itself to have a different ending than you have plotted, then you don't want that scene, no matter how inviting it may be.

Conversely, if it alters the plot of your story in a direction that you *would* want to go—if it creates later scenes that you would want to live out—then you might indeed want to add that scene. No matter how hard the scene itself is, you might want to choose it because it will get you where you want to go.

SCRIPT A HAPPY ENDING

Once, while I was doing a seminar on reaching goals and dreams, a lady asked if we could talk for a moment. When we sat down, she told me that she had dreamed of being a lawyer since she was a little girl. It seemed like the ideal profession for her. She said she would love the work and it would be a great way of helping people.

"What do you do now?" I asked.

"I work in the loan industry, but I hate it," she replied. "Every day I wish I were doing something different, especially practicing law. I'm grateful I have a good job, but it's not how I want to spend my life."

"Then why don't you become a lawyer?" I asked.

"Because I would have to go to three years of law school, and that would just be too long."

It was clear to me that this woman did not know how to *play the movie*. So I played it for her. I said, "Do you plan to be alive three years from now?"

"Well, I certainly hope so!" she replied.

"Then think about this. Three years from now will arrive, and you will be alive. So here's the question: On that day three years from now, do you want to have a law degree, enabling you to do something you love? Or do you want to still hate your life?"

"I never thought about it that way," she said. "It's not about three years seeming like a long time. It's about where I will be in three years if I don't do this."

She was catching on to the script of her movie. She could see that choosing to avoid law school was not just an isolated decision. It was only one scene, but the movie was going to keep playing regardless, and that scene would dictate the way it turned out. The movie is not optional, but the happy ending is. She could choose to be in a very different movie, one she would like. Or she could choose to be in one she did not like at all. It was up to her.

When we think of a difficult thing to do, such as getting an advanced degree, trimming the fat from an already lean corporate budget, or even changing careers, we often just think of the immediate comfort that comes from not doing it. We act as if the present is all there is, forgetting that the future is going to come no matter what we decide. Immediate relief from hard work is not the only consequence. By avoiding the immediate discomfort, you also sign up for the negative consequences residing within the future reality.

Playing the whole movie can save your life by preventing bad things from happening, and it can build your life by enabling you to see the good things that can happen. I have a friend who devotes a certain amount of his spare time to buying and fixing up rental properties. This is not as much fun as other things he could be doing with those free weekends. So what keeps him doing it? He told me that he plays the movie ten to fifteen years down the road. The mortgages will be almost paid off, the rents will have increased, and he will be retired. And by the end of the movie, he is doing a lot of fishing and golfing and not a lot of working, a scene he looks forward to.

SURVIVE THE SCARY SCENES

In addition to motivation, playing the movie provides successful leaders with another strategy common to all of them. They use it to live out the difficulties before they actually occur. In other words, they worry ahead of time, meaning they play the movie and then take active steps to make sure they are ready for unpleasant scenes when they arrive.

I had lunch one day with a déjà vu leader and friend who owns a highly successful construction business. "What are you working on now?" I asked.

"War games," he said.

"What?" I asked.

"We're having a week of what we call war games," he replied. "We play out future bad scenarios and make sure we're in a position to handle them. For example, what if interest rates go sky high in two years? What if land costs increase? What if there is a union strike? We look at what these would do to us as a company and make adjustments now that will allow us to survive them."

That's being a lot more active about the future than just making sure you have enough cash reserves, isn't it? No wonder this man has been so successful for so long. He will thrive in the tough times because he has already lived through them, theoretically, and survived by playing the movie.

When I conduct seminars on reaching goals, I often

have leaders isolate and plan the worst things they will have to face if they try to reach their goals. I have them play the movie ahead of time and devise a strategy to prepare for the worst scene before it hits.

GIVE AN OSCAR-WINNING PERFORMANCE

Plot a movie, a vision of your life, your career, your relationships, your finances, and so on. See it, plan it, and then evaluate each scene you write every day in light of where the movie is supposed to end. If you do that, and make sure that you include the right supporting cast along the way, I will be so happy when you get your Oscar for successful leadership and a life well lived. "Well done, good and faithful servant!" (Matthew 25:21).

And the cool thing is that the best reward is the life you will have built over time. That is the reality that will not only last for eternity, but will also give you abundance and fulfillment along the way. Choose the right scene at each pivotal moment, and you'll be the star in a great movie, one scene at a time.

4

PUT SUPERMAN OUT OF A JOB

THING FOUR

Déjà vu leaders continually ask themselves,
"What can I do to make this situation better?"

You've probably seen it played out on the screen many times. A runaway train is about to jump the tracks, sending hundreds hurtling to their deaths. A mother and her children are trapped on the top floor of their flame-engulfed apartment building. A bunch of machine gun-toting bad guys are about to rob the city bank. The scenarios change, but have a common theme: People are in deep trouble and need help—*fast!*

At the last possible moment, bursting out of the nearest phone booth in his blue leotard and red cape comes Superman, faster than a speeding bullet. You

can substitute your favorite good guy if you want to—
Spiderman, Batman, the Avenger, whomever. But the
result is always the same: When the superhero arrives,
the threat is disarmed, the crisis is averted, and lives are
saved.

Here's what I wonder when I see those old clips: Why
doesn't somebody else step up and do something to save
the day? It's like everybody else is powerless even to try
to intervene. The people seem resigned to the fact that
if Superman doesn't show up, they're all doomed. So
nobody even tries.

Déjà vu leaders do not reflect the paralysis of the
citizens of Metropolis. Rather, as our fourth principle
states,

---

*Déjà vu leaders continually ask themselves,
"What can I do to make this situation better?"*—

---

and then they do something. They tend to call on
themselves as the first source to correct difficult situations.
It doesn't matter whether they think they are to blame or

not. Even if someone else is at fault, they take initiative to address the problem and seek a solution. Whatever the answer may be, *déjà vu leaders make a move.*

SPRING INTO ACTION

We live out our lives in various contexts, circumstances, and environments. At any given moment, we find ourselves in many roles and relationships. While contexts change, the constant is who we are as people, our character, and how we express that character in the ways we live. The déjà vu leader tends to be consistent in living out the *get moving* approach in whatever setting he finds himself. In many different contexts, he practices ownership and responsibility, and therefore finds freedom and success.

A great majority of the problems we face as leaders are people problems. When there is a breach in a relationship, the déjà vu leader figures out what he can do to repair it. Instead of hoping that someone else will make the first move, the good leader might take the following actions as appropriate:

- Ask, "Is there anything in my attitudes or actions that have contributed to this problem? What can I do to change those?"

- Deal with their hurt and anger so their communication is more likely to help things rather than hurt.

- Ask, "How can I communicate to the other person that I see the role I have played in our problem?"

- Go and apologize.

- Go and confront.

- Go with an agenda of only listening and trying to understand how the other person has been hurt.

- Go and make amends.

- Get feedback from others on what ways they need to change, and then find out how to do it.

With people who are hurtful, angry, controlling, or have problems that affect you negatively, instead of letting your feelings depend on their moods or behaviors, *do something:*

- Go and make them aware of the problem.

- Ask if there is anything you can do to make it better.

- Set limits on your exposure to the problem, and let them know that you will not be around them as long as it is occurring.

- Offer to help them get help.

- Bring in others to help; perform an intervention of some sort if necessary.

- Get away if they are abusive, and make it clear that you will not be around until they get help.

- Take responsibility inside yourself for your reactions and the way you allow a problem person to get to you.

- Choose different and better reactions than the ways you have responded previously.

- Get help to respond differently.

- Manage your expectations.

- Love them instead of expecting things from them.

- Stop enabling the problem in whatever way you might be doing so.

- Do not depend on them for things they cannot give, such as approval, validation, or love.

- Enforce consequences.

Compare the people who actively do things in these examples with the ones who sit and complain, stuck in their misery and wishing that someone in particular or life in general were treating them differently. I have seen lives transformed when people begin to adopt the déjà vu leader's strategy of asking himself, "What can I do to make this better?"

GET OUT OF THE PHONE BOOTH

Recently I was talking to a friend of mine, Tony Thomopoulos, who became president of ABC Television. The story of how his career got started is a great example of how to be an active participant in the events that shape one's life.

He began in the proverbial mailroom. *He chose the mailroom* over more interesting positions because he knew that delivering the mail throughout the company would put him in contact with every department. He would meet all the people in the company, know what they did, understand all the jobs, and then be better equipped to work his way up.

He then set a goal to be involved in a certain division by a certain date. He did not limit himself to some narrow description of a job, but agreed with himself to take any position available just to get into that division. The heat was on for him to be active—pressure imposed by no one other than himself.

Through delivering the mail, he met employees in human resources and learned of an opportunity coming up in his targeted division—someone was needed to take over a position for just two weeks while an employee was on vacation. The hours, 4:30 to 8:30 in the morning, were such that he could take the temporary position and still keep his regular job.

He knew nothing about the work he would be doing in the temporary position, but that didn't stop him. He spent the weekend researching how he could do the best job possible in the short two weeks that he would be in that division. He arrived each morning at 3:30, an hour early, to prepare for his tasks. He found ways to benefit his boss instead of just trying to make himself look good. He truly served his boss. He added value to the division and to the company.

After two weeks, the boss was so impressed with how prepared Tony was and the job he was doing that he hired him away from the mailroom. My friend was now in the division of the company that he desired. From there he was picked up by the upper management, and the ball started rolling that placed him in the president's chair a handful of years later.

Luck? Providence? Certainly. As Tony said, "I can see that God was involved in every step." But it was the same God who gave us the parable of the talents. That story tells us that God's system requires a successful leader to behave exactly as my friend Tony did.

Do Something Super

Dig up your dream, but then ask yourself, "What do I need to do now? How can I improve my lot? What do I need to do to get where I want to be? What skills do I need to develop? What fears do I need to get past? Whom do I need to meet? How can I invest my talents?" Those questions address steps toward proactive initiation, which God's system demands of those who expect success.

Then He asks us to ask Him for His provision to open doors and make opportunities for that initiative to be exercised. We must pray, and *we must also act.*

If it takes money to make money (a common excuse), then go raise the money you need. Don't just sit there wishing for a bigger budget.

Do something. Make a move.

If the economy is lousy, don't wait for it to change. Gain a skill in a different field, look somewhere else, find another niche that is hot, enlarge your network or openness to other jobs, start your own service business, or *something.* Don't just sit around and wait.

As the great British actress Dame Flora Robinson said, "Ask God's blessing on your work. But don't ask Him to do it for you."

So get with the program! Be who God created you to be. Send Superman to the unemployment line. Get moving and *do something!*

5

EMBRACE YOUR INNER INSECT

THING FIVE
*Déjà vu leaders achieve big goals by
taking small steps over time.*

There was a point in my life when I faced what
seemed to be a very difficult task, and I really
did not know how I was going to accomplish it.
The task was to write a doctoral dissertation to complete
a PhD. Quite a large number of people complete their
graduate school coursework and never get their doctoral
degrees because they cannot complete a dissertation.
I could have been one of them. It is a huge, time-
consuming, labor-intensive process.

At that time in my life, I was the kind of person who
always got my work done, but I was not good at developing

61

a structured program to accomplish the many and varied tasks that a dissertation required. I simply didn't know where to start. So I did what I had learned to do whenever I don't know what to do: I prayed. I asked God to help me, because I did not have a chance of getting this thing done on my own. At some point I was led to open my Bible. Here is what I found:

> *Go to the ant, you sluggard;*
> *consider its ways and be wise!*
> *It has no commander,*
> *no overseer or ruler,*
> *yet it stores its provisions in summer*
> *and gathers its food at harvest.*
> Proverbs 6:6-8

I wondered how in the world this passage was going to help me with my dissertation. I noticed the word *sluggard,* which means indolent, adverse to activity, habitually lazy. I had always been extremely active, and I wasn't lazy. Then I noticed another meaning of the word: *causing little or no pain.* I began to see the point. My tendency was to choose paths that caused me little or no pain. In this situation, I was avoiding the pain of tackling the dissertation because the task seemed overwhelming. It was so painful to think about that mostly I didn't.

Then I considered the part of the passage about watching ants. Watch them? I always just sprayed them. Where do you watch ants? I didn't know. Then a friend bought me an ant farm. I felt a little silly, as most ant farms are probably purchased for eight-year-olds. But I set up the sand-filled glass container and poured in the ants. Of course, you can guess what happened. After some time had passed, an entire ant city had been built.

The reality was that many tiny ants had taken many tiny steps and voila! A city was built. It hit me hard.

This entire feat was really no more complex than one step at a time, one grain of sand at a time.

If an ant could do it, so could I.

Not too long after that, one small step at a time, a dissertation appeared in my hands. What seemed impossible for me had been done. How? Just like Henry Ford said: "Nothing is particularly hard if you divide it into small jobs."

What those ants taught me was one of the most important things I ever learned, and it is our fifth principle:

Déjà vu leaders achieve big goals
by taking small steps over time.

If I had examined the few significant things I had already accomplished in life, I would have seen that *they were done in the fashion of the ant as well.* It is true of all successful leaders. They all achieve their successes by embracing their inner insect and acting like an ant.

BUT I WANT IT *ALL!*

The biggest enemy of the small-steps-big-results principle is our craving for having it all. If the ant picks up a grain of sand, the city will be built. But if the ant looks at the grain and says, "That is not a city! What a waste of time!" there will be no city in the end. Perhaps you can identify with one or more of the following examples of all-or-nothing thinking:

- *We need to wipe out three years of losses by the end of this fiscal year.*

- *Skip the training. We need to get those new-hires on the phones right away.*

- *I have to lose twenty pounds in time for the annual meeting next weekend.*

- *If we don't hire sales reps in all eight territories right now, we'll lose ground to the competition.*

- *If I don't land a partnership in a year, I'm quitting.*

- *Sorry, honey, I have to work weekends or I won't earn my bonus.*

All-or-nothing thinking keeps people stuck in destructive ruts. All success is built and sustained just like a building is built, one brick at a time. But one brick seems too small and insignificant for all-or-nothing thinkers. They want it all, and one brick, one dollar, one pound, one new customer, is not enough for them.

Déjà vu leaders are different. They value the little increments, the tiny steps. Several years ago a friend of mine offered me an opportunity to buy into a business partnership. At the time I had my eye on some other investments that had bigger, more aggressive goals. This deal was slow and had a longer pay-down in smaller increments. The thing that led me to invest in this venture, however, was my friend showing me where he was in the deal. Having invested little by little, year after year, he had paid down the debt through his profits. By that time he was retired several times over, enjoying at a relatively young age the fruits of one brick at a time.

Many people have applied this principle to paying down their mortgages, college loans, and business debts. Talk to your loan officer and ask what happens if you put a little extra into each month's payment. If there is no prepayment penalty, you might be amazed at what a little more each month does to pay off the loan.

Does your office look like a mess, but the task of cleaning it up is way too big to tackle all at once? Spend ten minutes a day throwing things away, putting them in a give-away box, or straightening one work surface at a time. Do it every day for three months if necessary.

Are you out of shape? Start with ten minutes a day. Build up to fifteen, then twenty, until you reach your goal.

Always wanted to write a best-selling novel? Do what novelist John Grisham did. While working more than full time as an attorney, Grisham got up a little earlier each morning and wrote a little bit. Slowly, one page at a time, over a period of three years, *A Time to Kill* was completed. Since then he has sold tens of millions of books and is an incredible phenomenon of publishing history.

It is the method used by anyone who has ever accomplished anything substantial, because it is the way the universe is designed—things grow one little bit at a time. It all adds up to this:

Wanting it all keeps you from having any.

But I Want It *Now!*

Closely related to *I want it all* is its sister, *I want it now!* In my first book, *Changes That Heal,* I wrote that the shortcut is always the longest path. Often when people come to me with a problem, I will listen as they describe it and tell them that it can be resolved. There is hope. We know how to fix this.

"Great!" they say. "How long will it take?"

I tell them the amount of time I think will be required, and that they need to commit to a step-at-a-time process, often involving a long series of weekly sessions. Many commit to the process, and slowly a city of wellness is built. Since the process works, I feel so much hope when someone commits to it.

But some do not *build* a city of wellness because they want it *now.* When I tell them that what they want will come to them over time, these people say, "I can't wait that long." And off they go to someone who does short-term therapy or to a retreat or workshop that touts quick results. For some people, short-term therapy works okay. But often these people call me back after a while and acknowledge that they are ready to undertake a longer term process.

Wanting it now *keeps you from having it.* Taking the long road, one tiny step at a time, will actually get you there faster because you will not lose time by trying shortcuts. People who *want it now* face frequent discouragement—and actually lose time—because of their many false starts. Crash diets and get-rich-quick schemes usually waste precious time that could have been invested in a longer, more fruitful process. By obeying the natural growth order that God created, you will get in step with the universe, one grain of sand at a time.

WHAT ARE YOUR ANT FARMS?

Too often we get overwhelmed when the obstacles we see standing between us and our goals loom too enormous to tackle. We lament:

- *I have never succeeded before, in spite of many attempts.*

- *The distance from where I am now to where I want to be seems too great.*

- *The goal is just too big.*

- *Things are too messed up to have any hope.*

- *I don't have the skills.*

- *I don't have the resources, like money or help.*

- *I don't have the time to accomplish it.*

The one-grain-at-a-time approach applies to virtually every human endeavor. Here are some examples of how you can change your life and enjoy success as a leader like you never thought possible.

If your marriage is faltering, restore it one counseling session at a time, one act of kindness at a time, one example of not overreacting at a time, one bouquet of flowers at a time, one doing-something-unexpected-and-sacrificial at a time.

If your relationship with your teenager is strained, build it one moment of connection at a time.

If you are in sales, build a portfolio of clients one phone call at a time. Meet one prospect at a time. Sell one policy or widget at a time.

If you want to start a new company or grow the one you have, get one more customer at a time. Get an advanced degree one course at a time.

If you are depressed, get out of bed and do one small thing, like going to the park and walking. Or call a friend to do something different one night instead of staying passively at home. Take one step of journaling your thoughts and feelings for ten minutes a day and deciding to change one negative belief or thought.

As time goes on, you will succeed, and others will look at you and think, *I can't imagine how he or she did that! What an accomplishment!* Then, you can look at an ant and say, *Thanks!*

6

EARN A BLACK BELT IN HATE

THING SIX

*Déjà vu leaders develop the ability
to hate the right things well.*

It was a déjà vu moment. I had a new partner in a venture that I was really excited about. He was well regarded for his accomplishments in business, leadership, and philanthropic causes. I was impressed with his business background, as he had sold a company a few years before for more than half a billion dollars, making a huge profit in the process. He was smart, creative, and capable. I looked forward to learning much from seeing these attributes in action.

The déjà vu moment came when he requested a meeting as a result of a problem we discovered shortly after he joined the partnership. Our accountant found a debt owed by the partnership that had not been disclosed in the purchase. Since this kind of accounting event is not unusual, I didn't give it much thought. It was business as usual.

As we sat down I could tell that my new partner was not happy. "I don't mind problems, because business is about solving problems," he began. "But, I *hate* surprises. This new information was not disclosed to me in the purchase process. If I had known earlier, it would not have mattered. It is just a problem to be solved. But I was surprised by something I should have been told earlier. I don't want surprises."

I absolutely loved his attitude toward the situation. The thought went through my mind, *This is what successful leaders do. This is how they operate.* I thought at the moment of several other leaders who worked the very same way. It points out our sixth principle for successful leadership:

> *Déjà vu leaders develop the ability to hate the right things well.*

Hate That Makes Us Healthy

The principle of *hating well* seems like an oxymoron to most of us. We try to get over hatred because we have all seen the destruction that it causes. We usually think of hate as a problem to be solved.

In reality, though, hate is one of the most important aspects of being human. It is one of the most crucial ingredients of a good person's character. *What we hate* says a lot about who we are, what we value, what we care about. And *how we hate* says much about how we will succeed in business and life.

Basically, we are defined in part by what we love and what we hate. What we love shows what we will invest in, go for, move toward, give time and resources to, and orient ourselves toward with the best parts of who we are. You can tell a lot about people by what they love. You think differently, for example, about someone who "loves his job" as opposed to someone who "loves to win at all costs." What he loves gives you a window into his soul and lets you know what you can expect from him.

Likewise, we can know a lot about people by what

they hate. A person who hates hard work, for example, causes you to wonder. One who hates weakness would likely cause you to keep up your guard. Hate gives us a window into people's makeup in the same way love does.

What would you think, for example, about a person who said that he hates the following things: arrogance, lying, innocent people being hurt, harmful schemes, evil practices, telling lies about others, and things that stir up dissension among people? If a person's life demonstrated the truth of these claims, wouldn't you welcome that person as a coworker or business partner? Wouldn't it be easy to trust and depend on such a person?

You can depend on people who hate the items on the above list because they would endeavor to be the opposite of all those things in their dealings with you. They would stand up against those evils to protect you if others tried to inflict them on you. Proverbs 6:16-19 uses these same objects of hatred to describe what God himself hates. Such a person would make a good friend.

That is why I loved that moment with my new partner. When he said that he hates surprises, I learned a lot about him. I learned that he liked to deal with things in the open and that he would take active steps to put an end to the things he hates when they present themselves. My trust in him grew at that moment. I knew that when dealing with him I was always likely to get the whole picture because that is what he values. He hates anything less.

Our character is in some ways formed through a process of what we hate and move against. For example, if we hate duplicity, then we want to be different from duplicity. So we move toward being the opposite, which is a move toward being open and honest. Thus,

---

character is in part formed by what we hate,
because we move to be different from whatever that is.

HATE THAT PROTECTS AND DESTROYS

So the first thing that hate does for us is help us move against certain traits and issues, thus becoming different from them. We push away from attaching ourselves to the things we hate. Our hatred serves as a preventative force.

The second way hate benefits us is that it causes us to protect what we value. We hate it when things we love are threatened, so we move to protect them. In that way, hate is a protective emotion, urging us to stand for operating openly in the light.

The third way that hate is a good thing is the flip side of protection. Hate moves us to destroy bad things, which are often the things that threaten the good. The hate of evil protects the good not only by shielding it but also by cleansing the environment of the bad things that move against it. When we hate the evil around us, we move to get rid of it as an act of love. As the apostle Paul wrote, "Love must be sincere. Hate what is evil; cling to what is good" (Romans 12:9).

Hate is part of the immune system of your soul. In the same way that your body's immune system hates infection, the hate within your character identifies things in your life as evil. My friend had an active immune response to bad business dealings. He immediately moved against them, destroyed the threat, and protected the good things in the business relationship. That is exactly what hate is supposed to do.

HATE THAT SOLVES PROBLEMS

Déjà vu leaders hate in ways that *solve problems* as opposed to *creating problems*. That was one of the aspects I loved about my partner. He did not storm into the meeting enraged and yelling about the issue. He did not put anyone down or say anything hurtful. He went after the issue in a constructive fashion and solved the problem in the process.

> *Successful leaders move against the problem and show love and respect to the person at the same time.*

The person who does not hate well uses his hatred in a way that hurts things he cares about, such as his coworkers, his home, or even himself. It can be an ugly autoimmune disease of the soul and life. Non-successful people often fail because their hatred is not serving them or the things they care about. Instead, it is doing the opposite—attacking and destroying the very things they care about.

The difference between leaders who hate well and those who hate destructively lies in the difference between two kinds of hate: subjective and objective. Subjective hate is like any other state of subjective feelings. It is a pool of feelings and attitudes that resides in our soul, waiting for expression. It is not directed at anything specific or caused on any given day by any specific object. It is already there, sort of like an infection in the soul.

Subjective anger blasts other people, causes overreactions, dissensions, inability to resolve conflict, broken relationships, and many other relational diseases. It has a life of its own, and it runs counter to the goals of those who carry it around. As a result, they cannot succeed in leading others because the subjective hatred is working against their best efforts to make good things happen.

The answer is to make the subjective hatred objective.

> *Transform it to the kind of hate that solves problems,*
> *protects things that you value, and stands against*
> *the things that you do not want in your life and work.*

To do this requires finding the real objects of hate, making them specific, and using objective measures to enforce them productively, getting the rage out of the equation. Objective hate is laser-like in its precision when addressing what it is against, and very soft and intentional toward preserving the integrity and respect of the person, even if he or she is an offender.

HATE OR TOLERATE?

Choosing what you hate is serious business. What will you tolerate? What will you not? What will you work with and what will you absolutely under no conditions allow? What you do not hate well is going to find its way into your life.

Here are some tips that déjà vu leaders would offer:

Make your values intentional. Think about situations you have found to be hurtful, and what you should see as worthy of taking a stand against in order to protect what you love. Make a list of your values. Pray over them. Ask the déjà vu leaders you know what things in their lives are non-negotiable. Make sure that your list includes all the basics that you should take a stand against, like dishonesty, abuse, disrespect, control, and oppression.

Deal with your subjective hatred. Find the sources of your subjective hatred and make them objective. Put names and faces to the origins of your problematic feelings and attitudes. For example, if you have been hurt by an unreasonable boss in the past, do you feel subjective hate toward everyone in authority over you? Make that anger and hurt objective to the one person and offense that hurt you and do not generalize. Above all, seek healing and understanding for the parts of you that have been injured.

Mix hate with love and respect. A déjà vu leader shows up with what we call *integrated* character. In other words, when he brings his hate, he brings his love as well. His hate is integrated with his love and other values, such as respect for people, kindness, and forgiveness. That is how he can take a hard stand on a tough issue but remain loving and kind in the process.

Build your skills. Taking a stand against the things that destroy life can be tough if you have never learned the skills needed. Besides being strong enough inside, you might also need to learn some good conflict resolution or assertiveness skills. One thing that déjà vu leaders always do well is resolve conflict, and that means being honest and assertive without losing control, getting manipulated, or freaking out.

Whether you are going to hate is not an option. You have been created in the image of God to stand up for life and stand against things that destroy life. So when hateful things happen, you are going to have to respond. It is hardwired into you. But you must choose to respond in a constructive way. In the process, you will preserve most of the good things in your life, eliminate most of the destructive things, and experience much more success in your work and in your life.

7

FORGET ABOUT PLAYING FAIR

THING SEVEN

Déjà vu leaders give back better than they are given.

The business deal I was working on had taken substantial time and effort. There were several parties involved, and tons of work had been done to get the deal to where it was on this particular day. I had high hopes for success. Things looked good.

My meeting that day was supposed to be somewhat of a celebration. The man I was meeting with was the last pivotal person to make it all work. I had been getting to know him better, and I'd found him to be interesting, creative, and smart. So I had been looking forward to this day when we were to sign up to go the next step.

We were eating lunch and discussing all we had gone

through to get things to that point, and how happy we were that it had all worked out. That is when he said, "I am looking forward to working with you. You do your part, and I will do mine. Do me right, and I will do you right. But don't screw with me, or you won't like it. Mess with me, and I will mess with you right back. Treat me well and we'll be fine."

At that moment, I knew our deal was off. There was no way I was going forward with this man. Why? He just wanted to play fair, right? As long as I was treating him well, he would treat me well. But if I gave him less than he desired, then he was going to do the same back at me. Good for good, bad for bad. That's only fair. *But it will destroy every relationship in life, including your relationship with superiors, colleagues, subordinates, customers, vendors, and so on.*

So I told the man that our deal would not work for me, and I would not be able to move forward.

GOOD FOR GOOD AND BAD FOR BAD?

Playing fair in relationships will not work. I do not like

being in partnerships where the attitude is to give each other just what we deserve. That is certainly fair, but if you and I are business associates or coworkers, I want *better* than fair from you. I do not want to fail and have you get back at me in some way to even up the score.

Our seventh principle for successful leadership states:

Déjà vu leaders give back better than they are given.

That means that if I make a mistake, I want you to help me, not get back at me. If I fail, that is exactly when I need you to do better, not worse. If I do something wrong, I need for you to rise above it and show me, and be a force to get us on the right track, not to cause the situation to deteriorate into getting even.

I would want to do the same. If you made an error or did something detrimental to the relationship, I would want to help you see it, fix it, and do better. I would want to be a force to help raise you up, not drag you down. That is the only kind of partnership I want to be in.

THE FAULT WITH FAIRNESS

My potential partner was not a bad person. He was like most people we run into on a daily basis. They are fair as long as they are being treated fairly. They are loving as long as they are being loved. Playing fair works well—for a while.

The fault with fairness is that all it takes for any relationship to go sour is for one person not to perform, and then the other one will do the same. There is an interlocking dependency: *The other person must be good so I can be good.* But because no one ever performs perfectly, all it takes to drag a relationship down is one failure. Under the "play fair" system, deterioration is inevitable. See if these examples sound familiar:

- One person is a little withdrawn, so the other feels abandoned and give the silent treatment.

- One person is a little sarcastic, so the other one is sarcastic back.

- One person gets a little angry, so the other one snaps back.

Usually the one who began the cycle is not suddenly going to rise above it. More commonly he or she just hits the ball back over the net. The game is on, and there is no referee until the players undo the business deal, get called on the carpet by the boss, or land in court. The end result is that the relationship is over, at least for the moment. It has broken down. *There is no resolution,* just a smoldering need for revenge. Wrath and anger are vented, but nothing is gained, no problem is solved.

The sad reality is that this is the philosophy of the masses. Good and fair business partners split up every day. How often have you heard, "I can't believe they couldn't get together on that deal. They are both such good people; how could that have happened?" Fair is good. But fair does not work; so good people fail at relationships every day.

GETTING BEYOND FAIR

Here is Thing Seven expressed in three ways more eloquently than I could ever attempt:

If you love those who love you, what credit is that to you? Even "sinners" love those who love them. And if you do good to those who are good to you, what credit is that to you? Even "sinners" do that. And if you lend to those from whom you expect repayment, what credit is that to you? Even "sinners" lend to "sinners," expecting to be repaid in full. But love your enemies, do good to them, and lend to them without expecting to get anything back. Then your reward will be great, and you will be sons of the Most High, because he is kind to the ungrateful and wicked.
Luke 6:32-35

Do not repay anyone evil for evil.
Be careful to do what is right in the eyes of everybody.
If it is possible, as far as it depends on you,
live at peace with everyone.
Romans 12:17-18

Do not be overcome by evil,
but overcome evil with good.
Romans 12:21

People who succeed in leadership and life do not go around settling scores. They do not even keep score. They "run up the score" by doing good to others, even when others do not deserve it. They give them better than they are given. And as a result, they often bring the other person up to their level instead of being brought down to the level of the other. It is the law of love, changing things for the better.

Let's take a look at how déjà vu leaders make this principle work.

Get rid of anger. When you feel anger at someone who is only giving you what you deserve, there are two wrong ways to respond and one that is better.

The first wrong way to respond to your anger is not to feel it, to deny it, or not to allow it to tell you something is wrong. The second wrong way is to use anger to get back at those who wrong you—to put them down, hurt them, lash out, shame them, or manipulate them into improving. Neither of these ways can avert the impending dissolution of the relationship, and may indeed hasten it.

The right way is to use your anger to let the other person know there is a problem. Then, go and solve the problem by approaching the person in love, not anger, and facing the issue at hand. Fix problems in a way that treats the other person better than you were treated.

Ask yourself what is helpful. Giving back more than you were given will improve the relationship for both parties, not just for the offending one. The mature person in the relationship will ask,

---

How can I turn this around? How can I help? What does this person need? What could get him to a better place?

Giving back what is good is more helpful than allowing someone to get away with bad things.

Get past your own need. Successful leaders see life as a place to give, and as a by-product of giving, they receive back in the end. When a person takes the high road and helps a wayward coworker, spouse, or friend mature through love and enforcing limits, they often get a mature coworker, spouse, or friend as a reward for their sacrifice. By "losing our life" as Jesus puts it, we "gain it." But to demand it in the beginning, we lose it. The higher road that leads to a payoff is always the one that begins with the sacrifice of setting one's own needs aside. That may not be fair, but it's true.

Ask how you have contributed. Few things loosen gridlock in a relationship like asking the other person how you have hurt him or contributed to the problem. We cannot require maturity from the other person until we are being mature from our side. Going to him and showing that we care how our behavior affects him is a step in the right direction. *Overcome evil with good.*

Give the opposite. If someone tries to control you, do not control back. Give freedom instead. Give choices. If someone is perfectionistic or critical, do not criticize him for being critical. Don't agree with it; just accept it. Do not feed bad, destructive things, but instead sow exactly the opposite. Do not let the other person get away with hurting you, but avoid sowing more bad behavior into the relationship. That is self-defeating.

DON'T PLAY FAIR, PLAY RIGHT

Déjà vu leaders have transcended the need for revenge. Their first goal is to make things better for the other person or group. The other's benefit is their utmost concern. That does not mean they have no interest in their own benefits. It simply means that in their treatment of others, their goal is to do well by them *regardless of how they are treated.* They don't play fair; they play right.

Revenge is for immature people. Mature leaders know that ultimately the offending person is going to get what he deserves without anyone else bringing it about. God and the universe have a way of making that happen, as does the natural law of sowing and reaping. But even this ultimate payback is not something déjà vu leaders wish on another person, and that is the hallmark of their character. They truly want the best for others, even those who do not do well by them.

8

QUIT SELF-EXAGGERATING

Déjà vu leaders do not strive to be or to appear more than they really are.

Ryan was an accomplished business leader who worked for a Fortune 500 company. Young and energetic, he had climbed the corporate ladder quickly. After doing well with a few assignments in Japan and Australia, he was a rising commodity in his field. There were several reasons for his success, but in talking to him one day I saw one of the main ones.

I had heard the story of how in a short amount of time Ryan took an almost non-existent laundry soap business in China to one with sales of almost a billion dollars. It was an awesome accomplishment. Think about going into a country where you have never been, where you do not know the language, where you have no friends or support, and achieving such spectacular success. How do you do that? That's what I asked Ryan.

"I got a job on a rice farm," he said.

I was a little confused. "What does rice have to do with building a billion-dollar laundry detergent business?"

"Well, I thought that if I went to work on a rice farm and worked with the people day to day, I would learn how they used their soap," he said. "Then I could figure out what to do with the business."

"How did working with the people result in monster sales?" I asked.

"I learned that all the workers basically went to one spot to wash their clothes because the water was softer there," Ryan explained. "They made this inconvenient trip because the water in Chinese homes was hard. The softer water made for more suds and better cleaning, allowing them to use less soap."

"How did that knowledge create sales for you?" I asked. "You could not solve the water problem."

"Actually, I did," he said, "though I didn't change

the water. I took the information back to our research department, and we developed a detergent formula that created as many suds with hard water as it did with soft. So for the first time, they could do their wash at home. It was a revolution of sorts. Then we created ads showing all those bubbles from using the water in their own homes, and sales skyrocketed to $800 million."

Ryan's story reveals that the way to sell soap in China is to work on a rice farm. But the important question is, *What created the idea to work on a rice farm?* What caused my friend to do that? The answer: humility.

It was humility that made a billion dollars, not soap or rice. This simple but profound quality of déjà vu leaders, the eighth of the Nine Things, helps them succeed in business and life. The humility principle goes like this:

In other words, they are who they are. They know what they know and what they don't know. They know what they are good at and what they need to learn. If they need to find something out, they do so, rather than act like they know it already.

The Need to Be Greater Than We Are

Webster gives these definitions for the word *humble:* 1 : not proud or haughty : not arrogant or assertive; 2 : reflecting, expressing, or offered in a spirit of deference or submission (a *humble* apology); 3 a : ranking low in a hierarchy or scale : INSIGNIFICANT; UNPRETENTIOUS; b : not costly or luxurious (a *humble* contraption).

Through these definitions and others we can get a general feel for what it means to be humble, as opposed to proud. And most people can "smell" true humility as well as the stench of arrogance or pride that is its opposite. We know it when we see it.

But how do we understand humility in ways that we can put into practice as leaders? Ways that bring about fruit in our lives and our businesses? One simple guiding principle that encompasses many of the others is this:

> *Humility is not having a need to be or appear to be more than you are.*

A déjà vu leader is a human being like everyone else, avoiding the need to be more than that.

Just as humility sells soap, it can also build success in all areas of your life and leadership. Let's look at some important ways that humility contributes to success and how lacking it can guarantee failure.

EVERYBODY SCREWS UP

I was in the midst of one of the most difficult trials of my business life. An employee of mine had horribly mismanaged the company I owned while concealing from me the mounting debt his failures had caused. At the moment of my deepest despair, I got a providential call from one of my business mentors and heroes in life, a man who had amassed many successes in his business career.

I was a little embarrassed for him to know about the mess I had gotten myself into, but eventually I told him the whole sad story. When I finished, what he said changed the whole picture for me and played a big part in my being able to turn the situation around.

"We, including myself, have all been where you are," he began. "Anyone who builds something gets duped or fooled or surprised at least once. We have all had this experience where we don't know the next step or how to get out of trouble. But I'm confident that you'll figure it out. In fact, this is when you are at your best."

I was no smarter after that phone call, and I had no more answers than before. But knowing that *this is a part of the path of success, and that even very successful people go through loss, failure, and crises,* gave me courage and hope that I did not have before.

My mentor's humility was demonstrated in this fact: Even though he was enormously successful, *he accepted his own failures and mistakes, and even saw them as part of the process itself.* This is an important quality of déjà vu leaders—they are not surprised that they make mistakes; as a result, they can identify with others who do, give to them, and not judge them or wrongly judge themselves.

Identifying with other normal human beings who fail leads to a number of success patterns. Two of these are huge factors in achieving success in leadership:

1. Successful people show kindness, understanding, and help to others who fail.

2. Successful people are not derailed by their own failures; they accept them as a normal part of the process.

The first trait is certainly an incredible gift to give others. Over and over I have seen how déjà vu leaders extend themselves to serve others. They always tend to be givers of themselves. Success and giving are synonymous in many ways. Self-serving success always implodes. Self-centered lives always create self-destructing black holes. Always.

Humble givers also develop a lot of relational equity over time. They have extended themselves to understand and reach out to others, and as a result they are highly appreciated and loved. They create true networks of care in their lives. They experience high quality relationships as a result of their high quality giving and understanding.

The second point above is just as vital to success.

People who learn from failure are motivated to do better. Self-confidence does not come from seeing oneself as strong, without flaws, or above making mistakes. Self-confidence and belief in yourself come from accepting flaws and mistakes and realizing that you can go forward and grow past them, that you can learn from them.

EVERYBODY CAN LEARN FROM SCREW UPS

People who think they have it all together are infected with a terrible sickness, and they do not even know it. They flatter themselves, as David said, too much to see where they miss the mark (Psalm 36:2). In contrast, déjà vu leaders do not have the sickness of trying to preserve the view that that they are all good, either in their own minds or in the eyes of others, because they do not have such a view. Nor do they desire that others have that view of them.

Regarding their imperfections, these people do at least two things very well that build success, foster good relationships, and encourage learning, growth, and wisdom:

1. They admit it quickly when they are wrong.

2. They receive correction and confrontation from others well.

The first quality aids in learning and is always correlated with wisdom. We cannot grow and learn if we cannot admit our mistakes. How can we get better if we aren't willing to admit that anything is wrong? To see our own faults is a key to growing in wisdom and learning how to make things work.

Closely related to admitting our own mistakes is responding constructively when the news of our imperfections comes from others. The way of the déjà vu leader is to receive correction as a gift, not to be defensive. Defensiveness is the mark of a fool, as you certainly know from experience if you have ever given feedback to a defensive person. It is a maddening experience. Solomon said, "Whoever corrects a mocker invites insult; whoever rebukes a wicked man incurs abuse" (Proverbs 9:7).

A prideful spirit that resists correction makes for bad relationships. And past that, it makes for a lack of success in the endeavor of the defensive person. He is unable to grow and get past failure because he is closed off to the information that would help him.

Successful leaders fail just like everyone else. But it's the way they handle their failure and imperfections that sets them apart. Instead of feeling compelled to be seen as "right" or "good," they are interested in what is best, no matter who is right or wrong. You never hear words like *How dare you question me!* You hear *Oh, gosh. That's not good. Tell me more about how it felt to you,* or some similar response that lets you know they are not trying to defend themselves, but to help make it right.

GIVE IT UP AND SUCCEED MORE

Humility means giving up thinking that we know it all, giving up thinking we can do it all, giving up thinking we have to do it well all the time, giving up thinking that we are better than others when they do not do it well, giving up needing to be seen as right or good all the time, and giving up defensiveness. In all these cases, the way of the déjà vu leader is basically to be real.

The difference between déjà vu leaders and other so-called achievers is that they are successful in *all* of life. They are integrated, and unlike other people who accomplish things, they do not see success as *who* they are, lording it over others; they see themselves as people just like everyone else, and they do all they can to love and serve those around them. As a result, they succeed more.

Be a déjà vu leader and learn the way of humility. When you do, you will not only succeed more, but you will also keep your success. Here are a few tips on the humble ways of déjà vu leaders:

- Say you are sorry to your children, spouse, coworkers, customers, and other people in your life when you fail them.

- Get rid of any and all defensiveness when it occurs in you. What you are defending—the need to be more than you are—is not worth keeping.

- Serve the people "under" you in whatever

structures have placed you "over" them. In organizations where there are hierarchies, déjà vu leaders are as concerned with their relationship to the custodian as they are with their relationship to the CEO.

- Root out any attitude of entitlement. Embrace a spirit of gratitude for everything you have or any good treatment you get.

- When someone is hurt by you, listen. Try to understand what he or she is feeling and learn how you can make things better.

- Embrace your imperfections and the imperfections of others. Do not ever be surprised by them.

- Use failure as a teacher and a friend.

- *Be humble.*

9

IGNORE THE POPULARITY POLLS

THING NINE

*Déjà vu leaders do not make decisions
based on the fear of other people's reactions.*

My client Simon was as nice a guy as you would ever want to meet. He was always concerned about others, often reached out to them, and was sensitive to their feelings. As president of a sizable organization, he did many extra things for the employees. He spent large amounts of money on their personal growth and development, much more than the industry average. I was impressed by his commitment to people and their well-being. Because of his commitment to his employees, I would never have guessed that he would do what he did—an act which revealed him to be a déjà vu leader.

Simon had been hired to turn the company around. It had grown steadily for about twenty years when it hit a plateau. His job was to return the organization to the growth rates that it had experienced in its heyday.

But when he got into the midst of it all and began to study what was going on, he realized something. The solution to this company's stagnation was not going to be simply a matter of doing what they had been doing but doing it better, or even of adding radical innovations. He was going to have to restructure the entire operation from head to toe. That was the only way that the company would be able to adapt to the new market and meet its mission and purpose.

Simon was excited about the challenge, but there was a catch. The restructuring was going to be painful in two significant ways. First, many employees would lose their positions, get reassigned, be required to move, or even be laid off. Many people whom Simon cared for were going to be very upset and angry with him. Second, there were no short-term rewards to be had for Simon himself. The positive results of his actions would take a while to appear. Meanwhile, he would look like the bad guy for a least a few years. People would think he had failed miserably.

Knowing Simon, I did not expect the second hurdle, the temptation to worry about what others thought of his performance, to be a big one for him. He was not the type to seek admiration and flattery from others. But because he was such a people person, I did expect him to have a lot of conflict with the first hurdle. To cause so many people to be upset with him and put long-term relationships into serious conflict would be a very hard thing for him to do. As others-oriented as he was, I truly did not know if he could follow through, and I half expected a stall-out. What happened was exactly the opposite.

"Well, I announced the restructure," he told me. "It was the right thing to do, but it has caused a storm of relational fallout. A lot of people are mad at me now. So now I have to work things through with several people. I will spend hours and hours in one-on-one meetings with people I have known and worked with for years. It's not going to be fun."

I was stunned not only at his sense of resolve, but also with the fact that he had overcome the fear of other people's reactions. But in reality, *he never had that fear in the first place.* He accepted those reactions as a reality that would result from doing the right thing, but it never was a fear.

I have seen this characteristic consistently in truly successful leaders. As much as they love others and feel deeply the pain or distress that their decisions cause others, they operate by our ninth principle:

Déjà vu leaders do not make decisions based on the fear of other people's reactions.

Successful leaders are sensitive to the reactions of others, but when weighing whether or not a given course is right, whether or not someone else is going to like it is not a factor that carries any weight. Concern, yes; but weight, no. Déjà vu leaders decide to do what is right first and deal with the fallout second.

Let's look at some of the obstacles that oppose this vital principle of successful leadership.

"I Don't Want to Hurt His Feelings"

Think of situations where being overly concerned about hurting someone's feelings can cause a person to stall out or drag a bad thing on too long:

- Firing, laying off, demoting, or reassigning an employee

- Confronting someone

- Saying no to a request to do something that involves time, energy, money, or other resources

- Saying no to a request because it would violate one of your values

- Doing an intervention with someone because of her very destructive behavior

- Telling someone that he has overstayed his welcome

- Making someone aware of a flaw that she does not see in herself that is hurting her relationships with others

One of the important distinctions that déjà vu leaders make in these situations is between hurting someone and harming him. Hurt is a normal part of life. Our feelings can be hurt when we get confronted, for example. We have to swallow our pride and look at something negative about ourselves, and that hurts. But it hurts like surgery hurts: It's good for us. It hurts, but it does not injure or harm us.

Getting rejected is like that. Hearing "no" hurts at times, especially if we really want something. Failing or getting fired stings. But those things do not harm us. They are a part of life, and we learn from them if we are looking at life correctly. Hearing hard truth can actually help us. As Solomon says, "Wounds from a friend can be trusted" (Proverbs 27:6). Hurt does not mean harm.

Harm is when we injure people by doing destructive things to them. We do not offensively inflict injury on another person when we make a decision to do something that pains him if it is done for a purpose, or for one's own well-being. Learn the old saying, *I am not doing this to you. I am doing it for me.* That is not inflicting harm at all, even if the person on the receiving end acts as if it is.

"AFTER ALL I'VE DONE FOR YOU"

Another barrier that many people feel when making decisions is guilt. When they choose to do something for themselves, or make any kind of decision based on their conviction that it is the right thing to do, they sometimes feel as if they have done something bad because of people's adverse reactions.

The déjà vu leader may encounter guilt in situations like these:

- Accepting a well-earned promotion when a colleague with greater seniority will be passed over for the same position

- Laying off good employees who were simply the victims of a budget crunch

- Raising prices on faithful customers who will suffer from the increase

- Capping the commissions of a sales team

The responses you get may be along the lines of, "After all I've done for you and the company, this is the thanks I get?" or "I've done nothing wrong; why am I getting the shaft on this deal?" Stay fixed on your heading to do the right thing and do not allow the guilt messages to blow you off course.

"IF I DON'T GET WHAT I WANT, YOU'LL BE SORRY"

You usually do not see responsible people get angry and go on the attack just because they do not get what they want. But often you do see irresponsible people getting mad when they hear "no." If you give in to them, you will find out how true the words of Solomon are: "Do not rescue an angry man, lest you have to do it again tomorrow" (Proverbs 19:19, my paraphrase). In other words, if you give in once to someone's anger, get ready to do it again the next time you say no.

If you let the anger of other people decide your course of action for you, then you have just trained them in how to get what they want out of you. You have set yourself up for the same experience again. In addition, do you really want to give to someone who is only going to hate you if you don't? What kind of relationship is that?

If you are changing your course of action based on the fact that someone might get angry with you, you have chosen a flimsy foundation upon which to make a decision. You have lost control of yourself, and that is not what successful leaders do. They are not held hostage by anger.

"I Won't Like You"

Sometimes those who need to confront are afraid of not only a negative response such as anger or guilt, but the loss of something positive that they value too highly to risk. Simon, my businessman client, faced two possible scenarios, each of which was going to prove difficult.

One was that people would be upset, and the other was the loss of Simon's short-term rewards, such as people thinking he was doing a great job and looking up to him as a successful leader. For Simon, this temporary loss of a positive image was not a problem. But for some people, the fear of losing others' approval or love is a big value, even bigger than doing what they need to do to solve a problem.

Déjà vu leaders go against the odds if the odds are against what is right. They are willing to be the odd one, risking loss of approval in order to do the right thing. They understand that the approval of others does not go very far in making one truly fulfilled. It may be nice for a moment, but getting up every day and doing what you believe in is much more lasting.

Learn to Upset the Right People

I'm often asked by leaders, "How do you deal with controlling people?" My answer is that you convert them from being controlling to being frustrated. The only way people can be controlling is when we make them that way by doing what they want.

Here's what happens: They get angry, or use guilt, or get pushy, and we give in. Then we describe them as controlling. In reality, if we don't do what they want, we could not describe them as controlling. If we say no to them and do not do what they are demanding, they have no control over us. They are just frustrated. We have converted them from being controlling, to being frustrated.

Here are some examples of ways you can maintain the relationship by empathizing with them instead of letting them control you with their demands. You can say something like this:

"I'm so sorry it is frustrating you when I say no. I can see it is hard for you to accept."

"I'm sorry that it feels to you like I don't care. That must be difficult. But I so hope you can see that *do* I care."

"I'm sorry it is so frustrating to you that I am making this choice. I hope you can accept that I still care about you even though I have decided to this my way."

SET YOUR HEADING

To be a successful leader, you may not keep everyone around you happy. In fact, if you are successful in any arena of life, you are guaranteed to tick some people off! Jesus said it best: "Woe to you when all men speak well of you" (Luke 6:26). When *all* people speak well of you, it means that you are duplicitous and a people-pleaser. You cannot speak the truth, live out good values, and choose your own direction without disappointing some people.

The key is not to count your critics, but instead to weigh them. Forget the popularity polls. Don't try to avoid upsetting people; *just make sure you are upsetting the right ones.* If kind, loving, responsible, and honest people are upset with you, then you had better look at the choices you are making. But if controlling, hot and cold, irresponsible, or manipulative people are upset with you, then take courage—it might be a sign that you are doing the right thing and becoming a déjà vu leader!

CONCLUSION

BECOMING A DÉJÀ VU LEADER

It was one of my darkest days in college. My high hopes for a sports career were finally ended by a tendon injury. I had tried and failed to find a major that I could really sink my teeth into, but nothing grabbed me. Looming even larger was my worry about how success would come to me even if I did find a field that I liked. And to make my mood even darker, I had just broken up with a girlfriend with whom I was quite serious. I despaired that I would ever succeed in a meaningful career or a lasting relationship.

For some reason, that day I thought that I should look in the Bible, something I hadn't done much since arriving at college. When I opened the book, I came upon a verse that seemed to jump out at me. It was from a section where Jesus was saying that worrying about life (exactly what I was doing at the moment) does not get us very far in accomplishing what we desire. Instead, He pointed to a different path:

> *So do not worry, saying, "What shall we eat?" or "What shall we drink?" or "What shall we wear?" For the pagans run after all these things, and your heavenly Father knows that you need them. But seek first his kingdom and his righteousness, and all these things will be given you as well. Therefore do not worry about tomorrow, for tomorrow will worry about itself. Each day has enough trouble of its own.*
> Matthew 6:31-34

On that day, I did not know all that Jesus meant in those verses, but I did know that the way I was going about things was not working. So I decided to try it His way. I told Him that I wanted help, that my life was not working, and that I needed Him to show me the way to make it all come together. I guess you could call it the "leap of faith" that people talk about.

On that day I discovered four things that changed my life. They were the same four things that I have heard other people affirm countless times:

1. God is there to help us if we ask Him.

2. He not only helps us directly, He gives us others to help us.

3. He designed life to work according to certain truths and principles.

4. As we practice those truths and principles, good things are given.

That was a defining moment in my life. Turning my life and my future over to God and beginning to live and lead in the ways He directed me has led me into a life of fulfillment and fruitfulness beyond my greatest hopes.

I want to encourage you to employ these same four steps as you put the Nine Things into practice. I believe that God will help you. He will also give you people to help you, and He will reveal the truths you need to learn to put them into practice. Your job is to actively embrace these four steps as you learn the Nine Things.

Some of the items that follow may seem familiar to you because we have hit on them briefly in the previous chapters. But I list them here as stepping stones on the path of applying the Nine Things.

TWELVE STEPS TO APPLYING THE NINE THINGS

1. *Do Not Go It Alone*

As you look at the Nine Things and desire to practice them, look to wise, loving people to help you. Find a support group, a counselor, or a coach. There is no magic formula that tells you must get help. But there is a formula that says if you do not have help, you are not going to get as far (Ecclesiastes 4:9-12). So as Solomon wrote, and countless déjà vu leaders have proven, "Do not go it alone."

2. *Receive Wisdom*

We all have a lot to learn. Seek wisdom from those who know and have already done what you are seeking to do. Read, study, go to seminars, take classes, research, hang around with people who do it well. In short, take in all the information you can find that relates to what you want to do. Solomon said: "Wisdom is supreme; therefore get wisdom. Though it cost you all you have, get understanding" (Proverbs 4:7).

3. *Receive Feedback and Correction*

Wise people receive feedback well. If you had it all together, you would already be there. So just get comfortable with the fact that there are things about yourself and your ways that need correction. If you do that, you will be open to the answers when they come, and with each correction you will be one step closer to your goal.

4. *Find Models*

We cannot easily do what we have never seen done. Your models can be people you know well, like mentors, friends, or coaches. Or they can be people you "watch" through studying their stories and seeing how they behave. It is the watching and imitating that takes this step a little farther than step number one ("Do Not Go It Alone"). It is about seeing it done before you can do it.

5. *Review Your Patterns*

Is there a pattern to the way you fail? Look back at what has stopped you before and then use the quarantine principle explained in step ten that follows. Do not allow past patterns of failing to repeat themselves. Arming yourself against the patterns and triggers that set them off gives you protection when they come around again.

6. *Deal with Impediments*

There are times when our hurt, pain, or weakness gets in the way of our ability to practice the Nine Things. If you have clinical issues such as depression or anxiety, get help. By resolving those fears and hurts, you will find more freedom to practice and execute the Nine Things. See a good psychologist or counselor; join a group or a program.

7. Add Structure

Sometimes outside structure is needed to accomplish things for which you lack the discipline to accomplish alone. That's why people attend programs like Weight Watchers and Alcoholics Anonymous. Remember the axiom: If you have not had the discipline to do it on your own, you will not gain it by gritting your teeth and making one more try. Add the structure from the outside.

8. Practice, Practice, Practice, and Fail

Growth is a process. Give up your demand to have it all together right now. Failure is part of the process, and no one who ever got there did it without failing. A successful leader is one who steps out, fails, regroups, learns from the mistake, and tries again.

9. Change Your Beliefs

As you embark on this path of growth, you will find that forward movement exposes old belief systems that will try to deter you from your goal. But remember this: No matter how pervasive those beliefs are in your head, they have nothing to do with future reality. Listen to how you talk to yourself, then change each negative belief into a positive one that reflects the way you want to believe and can be translated into reality. Learn to talk back to the debilitating beliefs as you hear them come up in your head.

10. Quarantine Your Weaknesses

If you have a particular weakness or pattern that has derailed you in the past, make sure that you protect yourself from it. You must learn your triggers and make sure you are protected against them. Otherwise, they will lead you into the same failure as before.

11. Put Your Vision and Goals on Paper

If you have no plan or goals to get you somewhere, you will end up nowhere. But if you have written out your visions and goals, you are more likely to reach them. Write down the big vision and plan out small but achievable steps that will get you there. Put dates to each step. Ask others to hold you accountable to those steps and dates.

12. Pray, Pray, Pray

Jesus said that the one who asks, seeks, and knocks will

receive. Prayer is simple conversation with God, the Source of all that we need. If you ask Him, He will answer. And His answers are always for our good, even when they do not seem that way at the moment.

THE NINE THINGS ARE FOR EVERYONE

The principles we have discussed in these chapters are available to us all. Do not see leadership success as a goal that you cannot attain or a prize only for special or lucky people. Success is never embodied in a person, but in the ways of wisdom that transcend any one individual. What déjà vu leaders do is find those ways and practice them.

My hope is that you might realize that these ways are available to you as well. I encourage you to embark on a path of putting them into practice in your own life and becoming a déjà vu leader. If you stay on that path, I look forward to the time when I can meet you and see you do or say something that seems small and insignificant to you but seems vaguely familiar to me—like déjà vu.